Key Stage 1

Science Revision Guide

Penny Johnson

Schofield & Sims

Welcome to this book

This book will help you revise the science you have learnt in Years 1 and 2.

Green headings show you which topic is covered.

Illustrations and scientific diagrams help you to understand the topic.

Find out about words in **bold** by turning to the Glossary.

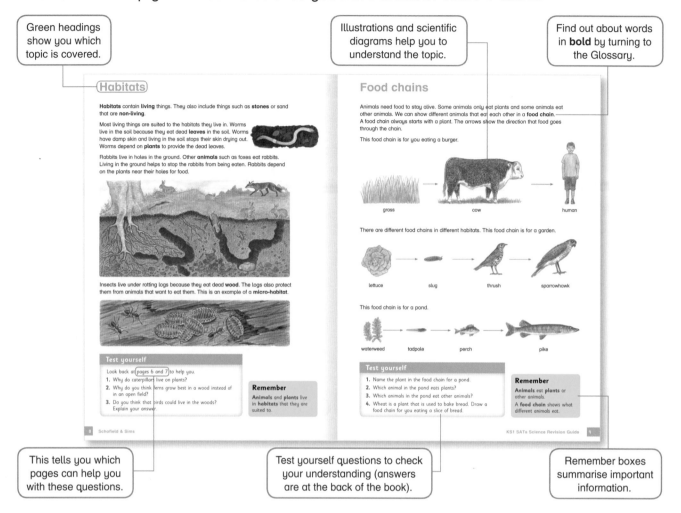

This tells you which pages can help you with these questions.

Test yourself questions to check your understanding (answers are at the back of the book).

Remember boxes summarise important information.

How to revise

- Turn to the topic and read about it.
- Read the Remember box and then cover it up. Can you remember what it says?
- Read the Test yourself questions and write your answers on a piece of paper.
- Check your answers against the right answers at the back of the book.
- If you got any answers wrong, read the topic again and have another go at the questions.
- If you got the answers right – well done! Move on to the next topic.

Tips for tests

- Always read the question carefully before you answer it.
- Have a go at as many questions as you can. If there is a question you really can't answer, just move on to the next one. You can always come back to it if you have time.
- If you are asked to explain something, you have to give a reason why it happens.
- Use scientific words if you can. For example, 'transparent' instead of 'see-through'.
- If you have time at the end, check through your work.

Contents

What is science?

Science is a way of finding out about ourselves and about the things around us.

What do scientists do?

Scientists investigate **living** things. They find out:

- about the parts of our bodies and how they work
- about **plants** and **animals**, and the similarities and differences between them
- how plants and animals **reproduce** (make **young**)
- how plants and animals live together in different places.

You can find out more about these things on pages 5 to 33.

Scientists **observe** the things around us, such as the weather and how this changes with the **seasons**.

You can find out more about these things on pages 34 to 35.

Scientists investigate **materials**. They find out:

- how to describe different materials
- how materials are used
- how materials can be tested and changed.

You can find out more about these things on pages 36 to 44.

How do scientists investigate things?

Scientists investigate things by collecting **evidence**. To do this scientists:

- observe things around them
- measure things
- record what they find out using words, drawings, tables or charts
- compare things in **fair tests**.

You can find out more about some of these things on pages 45 to 47.

Scientists think about the evidence they find. They:

- look for patterns in the evidence
- think about how they could have done the **investigation** in different ways
- explain to other people what they have found out.

Living and non-living things

There are many different kinds of living things. Plants and animals are living things. Living things can grow, move and reproduce.

Things such as **stones**, sand and pens are **non-living**. They do not move on their own. They do not grow or reproduce.

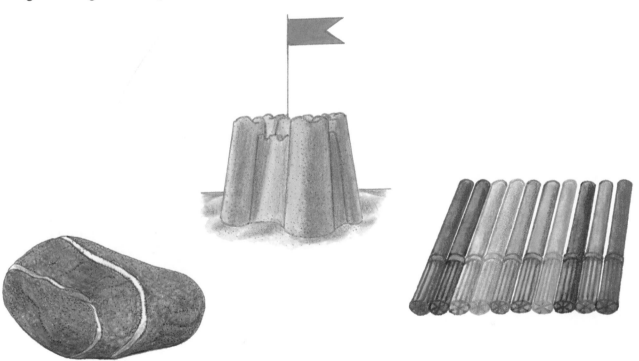

Non-living is not the same as 'dead'. A dead tree used to be alive, but a stone has never been alive.

Test yourself

1. Which word best describes a brick: 'non-living' or 'dead'?
2. Name three examples of living things.
3. Why is a stone a non-living thing? Explain your answer.

Remember

Animals and **plants** are **living** things. **Non-living** things have never been alive.

Where animals and plants live

In the park

The drawing shows part of a park. Lots of **plants** and **animals** live here. Different plants and animals live in different places in the park. The place where something lives is called its **habitat**. A very small habitat, such as a hole in a wall or a clump of grass, is called a **micro-habitat**.

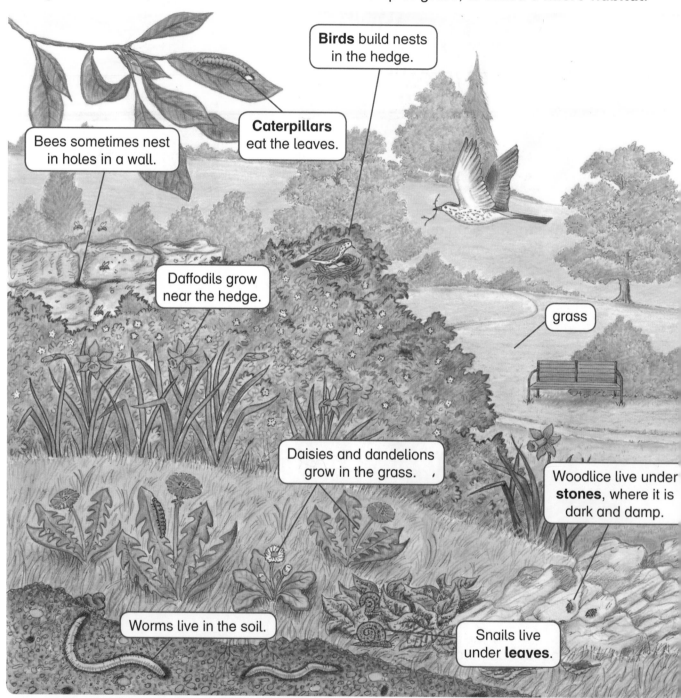

Birds build nests in the hedge.

Caterpillars eat the leaves.

Bees sometimes nest in holes in a wall.

Daffodils grow near the hedge.

grass

Daisies and dandelions grow in the grass.

Woodlice live under **stones**, where it is dark and damp.

Worms live in the soil.

Snails live under **leaves**.

Test yourself

1. Write down four plants that grow in the park.
2. Write down five animals that live in the park.
3. Write down one animal that lives in the soil in the park.

Remember

Different **plants** and **animals** live in different **habitats**.

In the wood

This drawing shows a wood. It is shady underneath the trees. There are different plants and animals in the wood compared to the park.

beech tree

Woodpeckers make nests in the trees.

oak tree

holly tree

Blackberry bushes grow under the trees.

Bluebells grow under the trees.

Lots of different insects live under rotting logs.

Squirrels live in the trees.

Rabbits live in holes in the ground.

Ferns grow where it is damp.

Test yourself

1. Write down four animals that live in the wood.
2. Write down five plants that grow in the wood.
3. Write down three animals that live in dark habitats.

Remember

Different **plants** and **animals** live in different places. A place like a wood can have dark, light, damp and dry parts.

Habitats

Habitats contain **living** things. They also include things such as **stones** or sand that are **non-living**.

Most living things are suited to the habitats they live in. Worms live in the soil because they eat dead **leaves** in the soil. Worms have damp skin and living in the soil stops their skin drying out. Worms depend on **plants** to provide the dead leaves.

Rabbits live in holes in the ground. Other **animals** such as foxes eat rabbits. Living in the ground helps to stop the rabbits from being eaten. Rabbits depend on the plants near their holes for food.

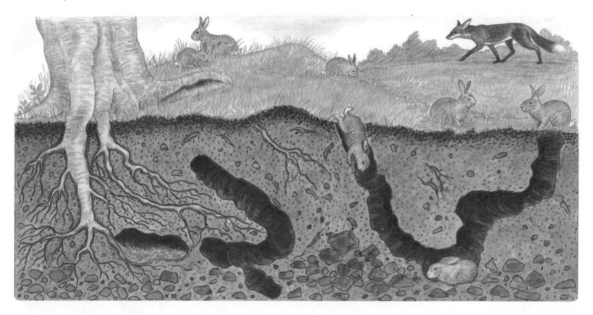

Insects live under rotting logs because they eat dead **wood**. The logs also protect them from animals that want to eat them. This is an example of a **micro-habitat**.

Test yourself

Look back at pages 6 and 7 to help you.

1. Why do caterpillars live on plants?
2. Why do you think ferns grow best in a wood instead of in an open field?
3. Do you think that birds could live in the woods? Explain your answer.

Remember

Animals and **plants** live in **habitats** that they are suited to.

Food chains

Animals need food to stay alive. Some animals only eat plants and some animals eat other animals. We can show different animals that eat each other in a **food chain**. A food chain always starts with a plant. The arrows show the direction that food goes through the chain.

This food chain is for you eating a burger.

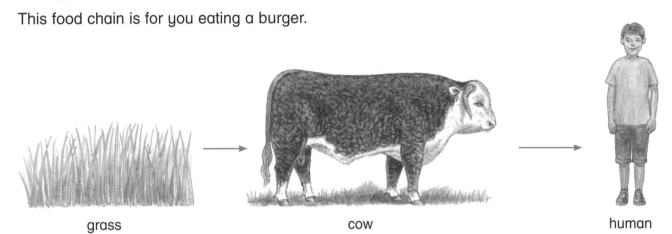

grass   cow   human

There are different food chains in different habitats. This food chain is for a garden.

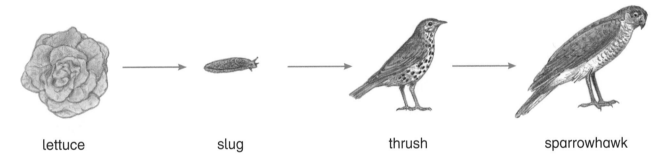

lettuce   slug   thrush   sparrowhawk

This food chain is for a pond.

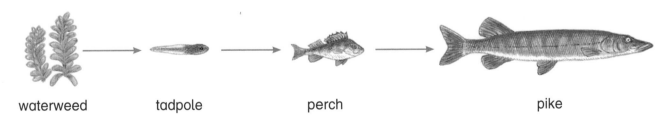

waterweed   tadpole   perch   pike

Test yourself

1. Name the plant in the food chain for a pond.
2. Which animal in the pond eats plants?
3. Which animals in the pond eat other animals?
4. Wheat is a plant that is used to bake bread. Draw a food chain for you eating a slice of bread.

Remember

Animals eat **plants** or other animals.

A **food chain** shows what different animals eat.

Plants

Plants are living things. Plants are all similar because they have green parts and leaves.

All plants grow.

A tiny seed can grow into a huge tree.

All plants reproduce.

Plants reproduce by making seeds. New plants grow from seeds.

Plants can also move.

They do not move around as animals do, but some plants can move parts of themselves. Some flowers close up at night.

Plants are different from each other in many ways.

Plants can:
- have different shaped leaves
- have different coloured flowers
- be different sizes.

For example, a cherry tree is much bigger than a daisy.

Test yourself

1. Write down the names of two different plants.
2. How do plants reproduce?
3. How are all plants similar to each other?
4. Write down two differences between a daisy and a cherry tree.

Remember

Plants are living things that grow, reproduce and move.

Plants are all similar because they have green parts and leaves.

Plant parts

Plants have different parts.

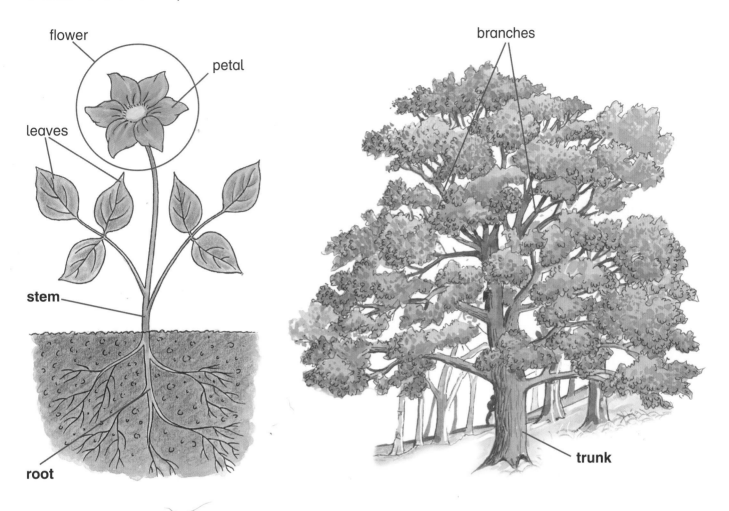

flower
petal
leaves
stem
root
branches
trunk

Not all plants have all of these parts. Some plants only have flowers at some times of the year. Some plants do not have leaves in **winter**. Moss plants do not have roots.

moss plant

Test yourself

1. Draw a picture of a plant.
   Write labels on your drawing to show what the different parts of the plant are called.
2. What plant parts do trees have that daisies do not?

Remember

Most **plants** have **flowers**, **leaves**, **roots** and **stems**.

Naming plants

Plants can be large or small. The largest plants are trees. We grow some plants in gardens because they look attractive. Other plants are only found in the wild.

Small plants

daisy   dandelion   buttercup

Daisy, dandelion and buttercup plants often grow in lawns.

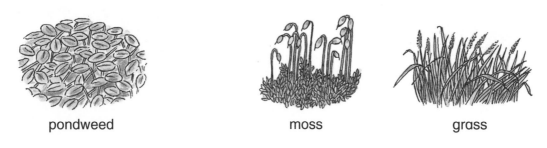

pondweed   moss   grass

Pondweed grows in water.   Moss plants grow in damp places.

carrot

We eat the **roots** of carrot plants.

daffodil

Daffodils flower in **spring**.

Trees

Some trees have **leaves** on all year round. These are **evergreen** trees.

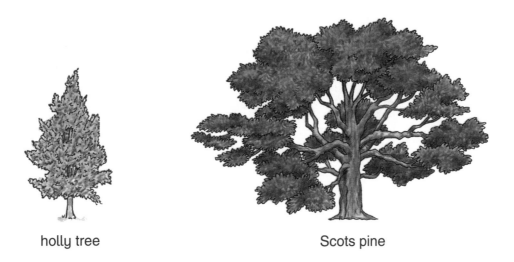

holly tree   Scots pine

Holly trees and Scots pine trees are evergreen.

Some trees lose all their leaves in winter. These are called **deciduous** trees.

oak tree in **summer**   oak tree in **winter**   horse chestnut tree

Horse chestnut and oak trees are deciduous.

Test yourself

1. Name one plant that we use for food.
2. Write down two plants that we often grow in gardens.
3. Is an oak tree deciduous or evergreen?
4. Will these trees lose their leaves in winter?
   a holly   **b** horse chestnut   **c** Scots pine

Remember

Deciduous trees lose their **leaves** in **winter**.

Evergreen trees keep their leaves in winter.

Seeds and bulbs

Seeds

Plants **reproduce** by making **seeds**. New plants grow from seeds.

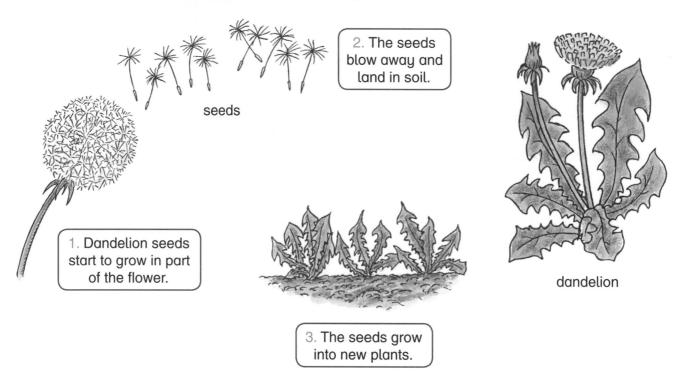

seeds

2. The seeds blow away and land in soil.

1. Dandelion seeds start to grow in part of the flower.

3. The seeds grow into new plants.

dandelion

Trees are flowering plants. They reproduce by making seeds.

2. The seed grows into a new tree.

1. The seed is inside the conker shell.

flower

horse chestnut tree

Some plants make **flowers** in the same year that they start to grow. Some plants, such as trees, have to grow for several years before they flower.

Many plants make **fruits** that have seeds inside them. Fruit seeds are sometimes called pips. Seeds and pips are different words for the same thing.

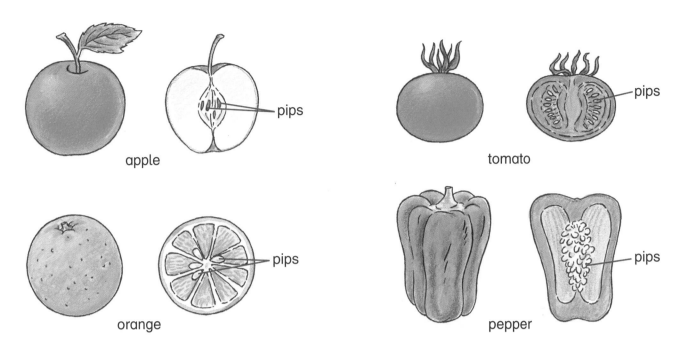

apple

tomato

orange

pepper

Bulbs

Plants such as tulips make seeds, but they can also grow from **bulbs**. Daffodils and food plants such as onions also grow from bulbs.

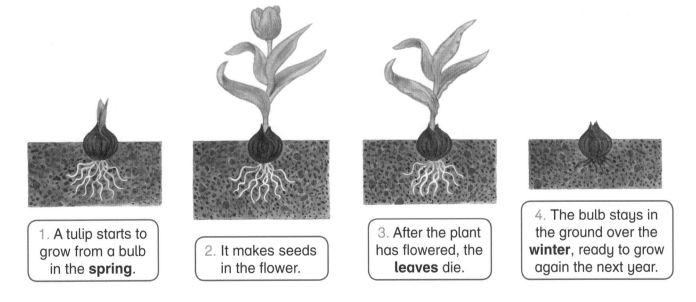

1. A tulip starts to grow from a bulb in the **spring**.

2. It makes seeds in the flower.

3. After the plant has flowered, the **leaves** die.

4. The bulb stays in the ground over the **winter**, ready to grow again the next year.

Test yourself

1. Write down two plants that can grow from seeds.
2. Write down three plants that can grow from bulbs.
3. What do new plants grow from?
4. Where do seeds grow inside a plant?
5. Which part of an apple will grow into a new plant?

Remember

Plants can grow from **seeds** or from **bulbs**.

Flowering plants make seeds.

Seeds grow into new plants.

Some seeds are inside **fruits**.

Growing seeds

Do seeds need water?

George wanted to find out if **seeds** need water to start growing. He planted two lots of cress seeds.

George watered this dish every day.

George did not water this dish at all.

This drawing shows George's seeds one week later.

George's **investigation** showed that seeds need water to start growing. It was a **fair test** because he used the same kind of seeds in both dishes and kept them in the same place.

Do seeds need soil?

Emily wanted to find out if seeds need soil to start growing. This is what she did.

| soil | sand | wet paper towel |

Emily watered all her containers. One week later they looked like this.

Her investigation shows that seeds do not have to be in soil to start growing.

Do seeds need light to start growing?

Isha wanted to find out if seeds need light to start growing.

Isha put this dish on a windowsill.   Isha put this dish in a cupboard.

 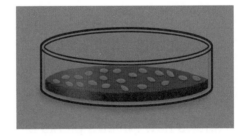

Isha watered all her containers. One week later, her seeds looked like this.

Isha's investigation shows that seeds do not need light to start growing.

Test yourself

1. What do seeds need to start growing?
2. Explain why Emily's investigation was a fair test.

Remember

Seeds need water to start growing. They do not have to be planted in soil.

Growing plants

Plants are living things. They need certain things to help them to grow.

Tom's investigation

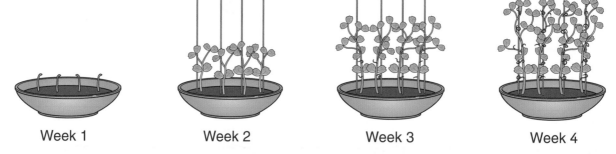

Week 1   Week 2   Week 3   Week 4

Tom observed some plants as they grew. He recorded his results in a table.

The table shows that plants get taller when they grow, and they get more **leaves**.

Each **stem** also gets wider.

Time	Height of plant	Number of leaves
Week 1	3 cm	0
Week 2	8 cm	6
Week 3	12 cm	12
Week 4	15 cm	14

Finley's investigation

Finley wanted to find out if plants need water to grow.

He put some plants in two pots and left them on the windowsill. He watered the plants in one pot every day. He did not water the other plants.

This picture shows how Finley's plants looked after two weeks.

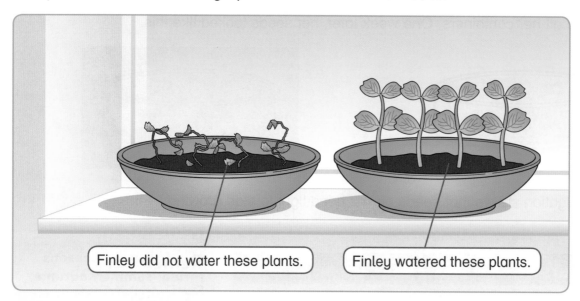

Finley did not water these plants.   Finley watered these plants.

Finley's **investigation** shows that plants need water to grow.

Plants also need to be kept warm, but not too hot.

Anya's investigation

Anya wanted to find out if plants need light to grow.

She planted some pea plants in two pots. She put one pot on the windowsill and left the other pot in a dark cupboard.

Anya watered the plants every day. After two weeks, her plants looked like this.

 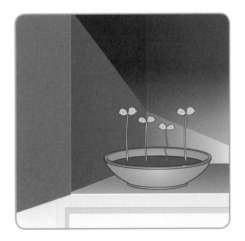

The plants on the windowsill had more leaves and thicker stems. They were healthy. The plants in the cupboard had grown very tall and thin. They did not have many leaves. They were not healthy. If plants are kept in the dark for a long time they will die.

Anya's investigation showed that plants need light to grow well. Anya did a **fair test**, because she only changed one thing (the amount of light).

Test yourself

1. Write down three things that plants need to grow.
2. How does a plant change when it grows?
3. What do plants look like if they have been kept in the dark?
4. What do plants look like if they have not been given any water for two weeks?
5. Explain why Finley's investigation was a fair test.

Remember

Plants need water, light and a suitable temperature to grow.

You can do **investigations** to find out what plants need.

An investigation should be a **fair test**, where you only change one thing.

Animals

Animals are **living** things. Animals are all similar because they can all move around. Many animals are similar to each other because they have eyes and legs.

All animals grow.

Animals are small when they are born. They grow bigger and bigger until they are **adults**.

All animals move.

Animals can move around. Animals need to move around to find food.

All animals **reproduce**.

Animals reproduce when they make new animals like themselves.

Animals are different from each other in many ways.

Animals can:
- have legs, wings or **fins**
- live in water or live on land
- have fur, feathers or **scales**
- be different shapes and sizes.

Common animals

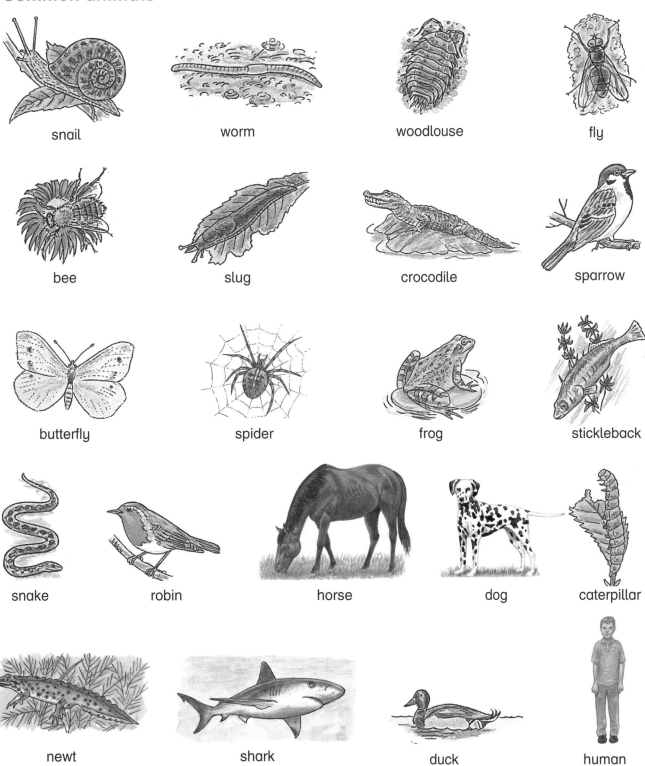

snail

worm

woodlouse

fly

bee

slug

crocodile

sparrow

butterfly

spider

frog

stickleback

snake

robin

horse

dog

caterpillar

newt

shark

duck

human

Test yourself

1. Write down the names of four different animals.
2. Write down three animals that have feathers.
3. Write down two animals that have fins.
4. How are all animals similar to each other?
5. Write down two differences between humans and crocodiles.

Remember

Animals are **living** things that grow, **reproduce** and move.

Animal bodies and groups

Animal bodies

Animals have lots of different body parts. Not all animals have the same kinds of body parts.

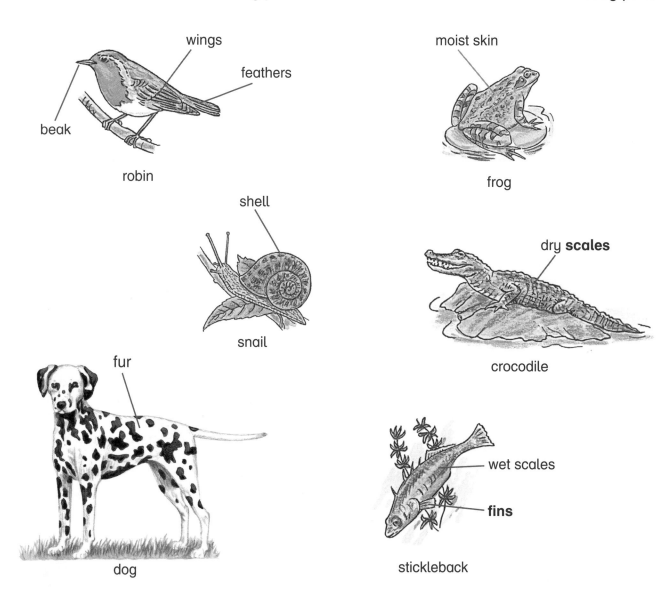

Animal groups

Scientists put animals into groups. All animals in a group are similar in some ways. They can be grouped by how they look.

Humans, dogs and horses are **mammals**. Mammals all have hair or fur.

Robins and ducks are **birds**. Birds all have beaks, wings and feathers.

Sticklebacks and sharks are **fish**. Fish all have fins and wet scales.

Crocodiles and snakes are **reptiles**. Reptiles all have dry scales.

Frogs and newts are **amphibians**. Amphibians all have moist skin.

Some animals such as snails, worms and insects, do not belong to any of these groups.

Animals can also be put into groups according to what they eat.

Herbivores are animals that only eat **plants**. Horses are herbivores.

horse

bee

snail

Carnivores are animals that only eat other animals. Cats and sharks are carnivores.

frog

shark

cat

Omnivores eat both plants and other animals. Humans and dogs are omnivores.

human

dog

fox

Test yourself

1. Name two animals that are reptiles.
2. Name two animals that are amphibians.
3. How are humans similar to dogs?
4. What do omnivores eat?
5. Are these animals herbivores, carnivores or omnivores?
   a Cows eat grass.
   b Robins eat insects, worms, fruit and seeds.
   c Sharks eat other fish.

Remember

All **animals** in a group are similar in some ways. Animals can be grouped by how they look or what they eat.

Herbivores only eat **plants**. **Carnivores** only eat other animals. **Omnivores** eat plants and animals.

Animal young

All animals **reproduce** by having **young**, which will grow up to be animals like themselves. **Humans** have babies, but some animals produce young in different ways.

Animal babies that look like small adults

Mammals such as cats, dogs, sheep and cows have baby animals that look like small **adults**. These baby animals need to be looked after by their parents.

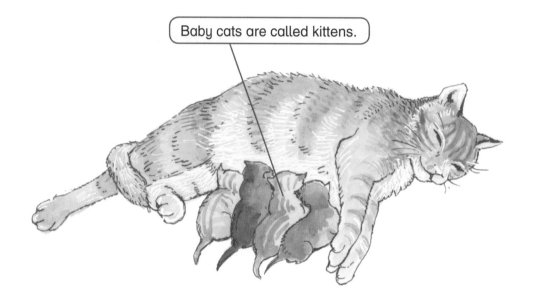

Baby cats are called kittens.

A baby cow is called a calf.

Animals that lay eggs

Birds lay **eggs**. They sit on the eggs to keep them warm while the baby birds grow inside. A baby bird hatches from each egg. The parent birds bring food to their babies.

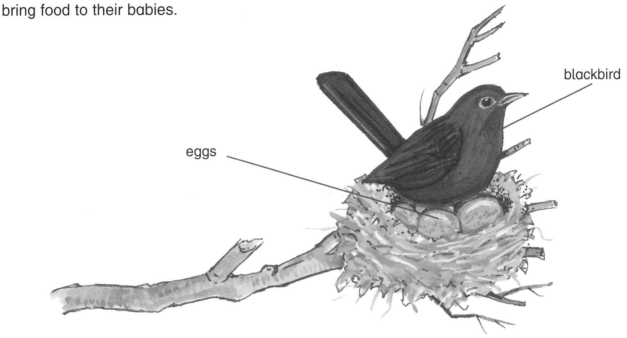

blackbird

eggs

Fish lay eggs in water and so do **amphibians**. Fish eggs and frog eggs are like little blobs of jelly. Fish and frogs do not look after their babies.

Test yourself

1. What is a baby cow called?
2. Which groups of animals lay eggs in water?
3. Name two animals that look after their babies?

Remember

Birds lay **eggs** and look after their **young**.

Fish and **amphibians** lay eggs in water. Fish and most amphibians do not look after their young.

Animals growing up

Baby **mammals** look like their parents, but are smaller. As they grow up, they get bigger and they may change a little bit.

Human babies look like small people and grow for about 18 years.

Baby pandas also look like their parents, but are smaller.

Baby **birds** do not look quite like their parents to start with. Baby ducks and flamingos only look a little bit like their parents.

Some baby animals look completely different from their parents to start with. Their bodies go through very big changes as they grow up.

Tadpole to frog

1. A frog's **egg**

2. The egg turns into a **tadpole**, which can swim around.

3. The tadpole grows legs.

4. The tadpole loses its tail and turns into a small frog.

5. The frog grows bigger until it is an **adult**. Now it can produce **young** of its own.

Caterpillar to butterfly

1. Butterfly eggs

2. A **caterpillar** comes out of the egg.

3. The caterpillar eats **leaves** and grows bigger.

4. The caterpillar wraps itself in a **chrysalis**. Inside the chrysalis its body is changing.

5. The caterpillar has changed into a butterfly. The butterfly can lay eggs to produce more young.

Test yourself

1. Which baby animals look like their parents, but are smaller?
2. Which baby animals look a little bit like their parents?
3. Which baby animals look very different from their parents?
4. What does a tadpole turn into when it grows up?
5. What does a caterpillar turn into when it grows up?

Remember

Some baby **animals** look like their parents.

Some baby animals do not look like their parents and change as they grow up.

Body parts

You are a **human**. All humans have bodies with similar parts. Your arms and legs help you to move around and explore.

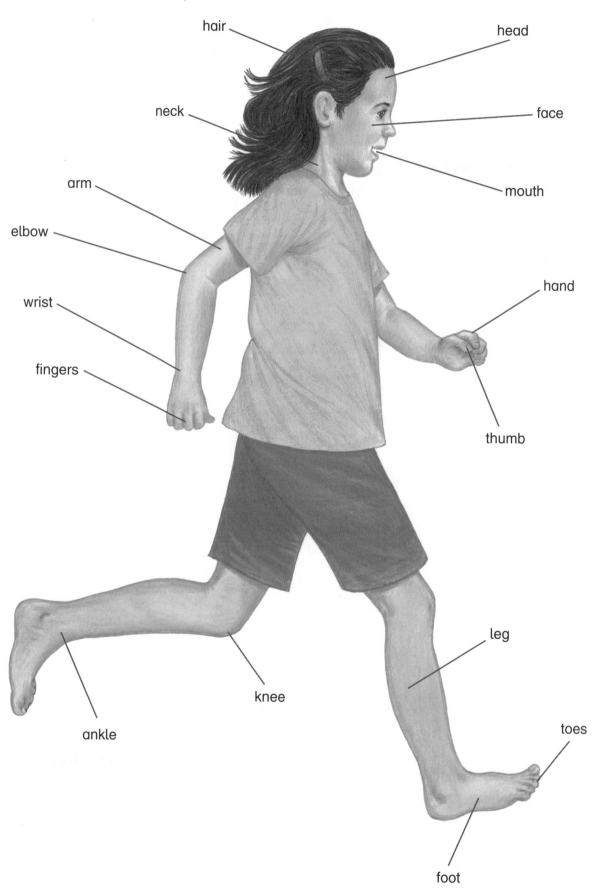

hair

head

neck

face

mouth

arm

elbow

wrist

hand

fingers

thumb

knee

leg

ankle

toes

foot

Senses

You have **senses** that allow you to find out about the world.

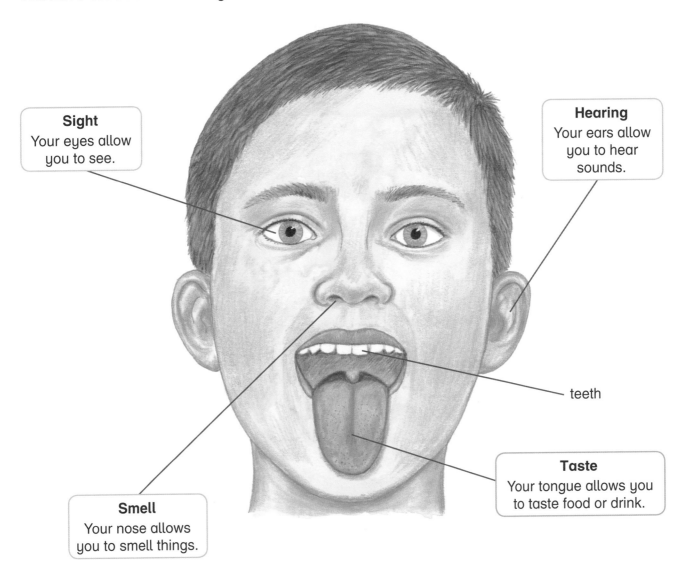

Sight
Your eyes allow you to see.

Hearing
Your ears allow you to hear sounds.

teeth

Taste
Your tongue allows you to taste food or drink.

Smell
Your nose allows you to smell things.

Touch
Your skin allows you to feel things. All the skin on your body can feel things, but your hands are very good at feeling.

Test yourself

1. Write down five different parts of your body.
2. What are the five senses?
3. Which part of your body allows you to feel things?

Remember

All **humans** have similar body parts.

Your **senses** are **sight**, **hearing**, **smell**, **taste** and **touch**.

Growing up

You started your life as a baby. Your body changed as you got older and it will keep on changing until you are an **adult**.

A new baby cannot do anything for itself. It needs to be looked after by its parents or other adults.

When the baby is older, it can feed itself and move around. Its parents or other carers still need to give it food and keep it clean.

A toddler can walk and talk.

You get taller and heavier as you get older. When you are an adult you can have babies of your own.

Children 5 years

Children 10 years

Teenagers 15 years

Adults 20 years

Remember

Humans change as they get older.

Children need to be looked after by their parents or carers.

Test yourself

1. Why does a baby need to be looked after?

2. Write down three things that you can do, but a baby cannot do.

3. How do your parents or carers look after you?

4. How will you change as you get older? Write down as many ways as you can.

5. How will you stay the same as you get older?

Keeping healthy

All **animals** need food and water to stay alive. They also need air to breathe.

Food

There are many different kinds of food. **Humans** need to eat a variety of foods to stay healthy.

In order to grow up healthy you need to eat lots of these foods.

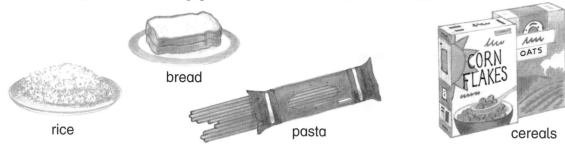

bread

rice

pasta

cereals

You need to eat plenty of **fruit** and vegetables.

apple   pear   bananas   tomato   apricot   strawberries   orange

carrots   broccoli   peas   beans   cabbage

You need to eat some of these foods to stay healthy, but not too much.

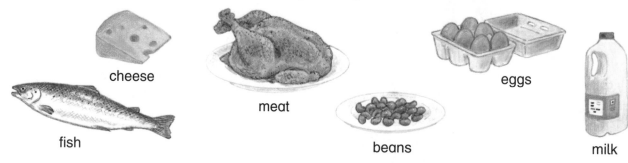

cheese

fish

meat

beans

eggs

milk

Some foods and drinks that we like are not very good for us, but it is all right to eat or drink a little of them.

ice cream   chocolate   fizzy drinks

Exercise

You also need to **exercise** to stay healthy.

Running exercises your legs.

Throwing exercises your arms.

Exercise can make you feel hot and tired, but it is good for your body. You need some exercise every day to stay healthy.

Hygiene

Hygiene means keeping yourself clean. This is important to help you to stay healthy.

You need to:
- wash your hands when they are dirty and always before eating food
- clean your teeth after breakfast and before going to bed
- shower or have a bath regularly.

Test yourself

1. What will happen to you if you do not eat or drink?
2. Write down three foods you need to eat a lot of.
3. Write down three foods that you should not eat very much of.
4. What do you need to do to stay healthy?
5. What do you feel like after you have been running?
6. Think about the foods you normally eat.
   a What should you eat more of to stay healthy?
   b What should you eat less of to stay healthy?

Remember

Humans need food and water to stay alive.

There are many different kinds of food.

You need to eat a variety of foods and **exercise** every day to stay healthy.

Changing seasons

We have four **seasons** in the UK. How long we have daylight for each day changes with the seasons and the weather is usually different.

In **winter** the days are short. In the middle of winter there are less than eight hours of daylight.

The weather is usually colder and wetter and it may snow. **Deciduous** trees have no **leaves**.

In **spring** the days start to get longer and the weather becomes warmer. There is a lot of rain. Many **plants** start to grow.

In **summer** the days are longer. In the middle of summer there can be 17 hours of daylight. The weather is warm or hot and there may not be much rain. Trees have all their leaves and many plants are growing and flowering.

It is not safe to look directly at the sun, even if you are wearing dark glasses. Looking at the sun can hurt your eyes.

In **autumn** the days start to be shorter again. The weather becomes colder and there may be more rain. Deciduous trees lose their leaves and many plants die down or stop growing.

Test yourself

1. In which season are there the most hours of daylight?
2. Which is the coldest season?
3. Which is the hottest season?
4. In which season do the trees start to lose their leaves?

Remember

The UK has four **seasons**: **spring**, **summer**, **autumn**, and **winter**. The weather and length of daylight changes in each season.

Materials and objects

There are lots of different **materials** all around us. Materials are used to make things.

Most materials are used to make different things.

Wood comes from trees. It can be cut into shapes. It can be painted or polished.

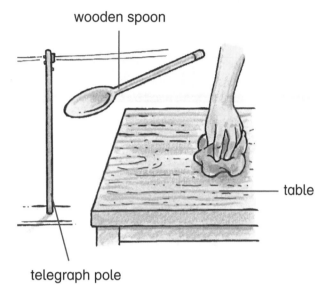

wooden spoon

table

telegraph pole

Plastic can be made into many different shapes.

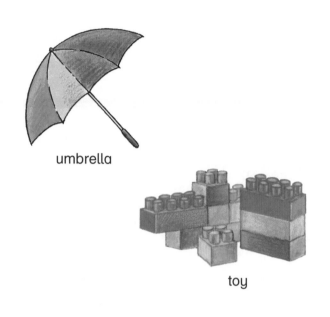

umbrella

toy

Metal can be made into different shapes. It can be painted or polished.

metal

saucepan

car

Glass is **transparent** (see-through).

window

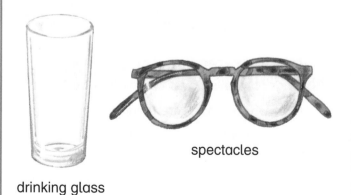

spectacles

drinking glass

Stone is dug up from the ground. It can be cut into shapes and smoothed and polished.

polished stone

buildings

Cotton comes from **plants**. It can be woven into cloth. **Wool** comes from sheep and can be woven or knitted into cloth.

cotton plant

cotton T-shirt

Paper and **cardboard** are made from **wood**.

book

cardboard box

Pottery is made from **clay**.

plates

mug

Sometimes the same kind of object can be made from different materials:

- spoons can be made from wood, metal or plastic
- chairs can be made from wood, metal or plastic or a combination of these materials
- cups and plates can be made from pottery, metal or plastic.

Test yourself

1. Write down three things that can be made from metal.
2. Write down three things that can be made from plastic.
3. Write down two things that can be made into cloth.
4. Write down three materials that can be used to make plates.
5. Write down three materials that can be made from living things.

Remember

The things around us are made from different **materials**.

Some materials can be used to make different things.

Some things can be made out of different materials.

Describing materials

There are lots of different **materials** all around us. We can describe what different materials are like.

Wool and **fabric** are soft.

Metals and **stones** are hard.

Stones and **rocks** are rough.

Glass is smooth.

Metal is shiny.

Clay is dull.

Paper is bendy.

Wood is stiff.

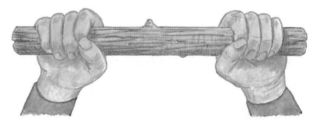

Glass is **transparent** (see-through).

Brick is **opaque** (not see-through).

Rubber bands are stretchy.

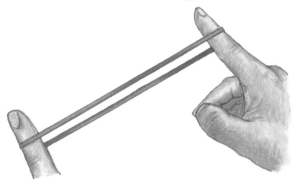

Wood is not stretchy.

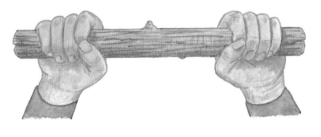

Cloth is **absorbent** (takes in water).

Metal is not absorbent.

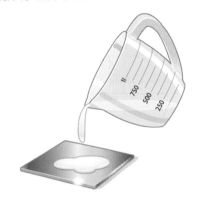

Plastic is **waterproof**.

Paper is not waterproof.

You can use more than one word to describe some materials. Wool is soft and bendy and not waterproof.

You can also group materials depending on their properties. For example, glass and some kinds of plastic are transparent. Paper, wool and cotton are all bendy.

Test yourself

1. Write down as many words as you can to describe this gold ring.
2. Write down as many words as you can to describe glass.
3. Write down as many words as you can to describe stone.
4. Write down three materials that are hard.
5. Write down three materials that are waterproof.

Remember

There are lots of different **materials** around us. We can describe what materials are like.

Choosing materials

Everything around us is made from **materials**. If we make something, we need to choose the right material.

Towels are made from **cotton** because it is soft and it soaks up water.

Jumpers are made from **wool** because it is soft and keeps us warm.

Windows are made from **glass** because it is **transparent** and **waterproof**.

Saucepans are made from **metal** because it is strong and waterproof.

The saucepan handle is made from **plastic** to make it more comfortable to hold.

Mugs and plates are made from **pottery**, because it is hard, stiff and waterproof.

Knives and spoons are made from metal because it is stiff and hard.

Cupboards and doors are made from **wood** because it is strong and stiff.

Bottles are made from plastic because it is light and transparent, so you can see how much liquid is left.

Different metals for different jobs

Metal is used to make lots of things. We use different kinds of metal for different jobs.

Gold is used for jewellery because it is shiny and looks beautiful.

This bridge is made of iron because iron is strong.

Comparing materials

Sometimes different materials can be used for the same job. Plastic plates are used for picnics as they will not break if they are dropped. Pottery is used for normal plates, because it looks more attractive. **Paper** plates are sometimes used at parties, because they are very cheap when you need a lot of them. They can also be thrown away afterwards instead of needing to be washed.

Test yourself

1. Why are the kitchen cupboards on page 40 made from wood?
2. Why do you think the table on page 40 is made from wood?
3. Why is a scarf made from wool?
4. Why are towels made from fabric?
5. Why do you think curtains are made from fabric?
6. Why are some bridges made from iron?

Remember

Different things are made from different **materials**. We need to choose the best materials to make different things.

Testing materials

If you want to make something, you may need to test different **materials** to find out which is the best one to use.

Which fabrics are waterproof?

Oliver and Zoë wanted to make a **waterproof** coat for their dog. They tested different **fabrics** to find out which ones were waterproof.

Zoë counted the number of drops of water that fell onto the plate in one minute.

Oliver and Zoë did the same thing again with other kinds of fabric. They made sure it was a **fair test** by:

- using the same amount of water each time
- counting the number of drops in one minute for each fabric
- only changing the material they were testing.

The **block diagram** shows their results.

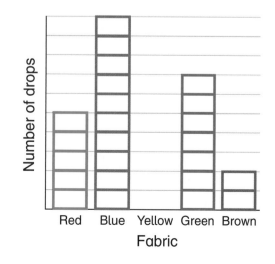

Which kind of stick is strongest?

Molly wanted some sticks to hold up her **plants** in the garden.

She wanted to find out which kind of stick was the strongest, so she tested the sticks like this. She kept adding weights to the bag until the stick broke. Molly made sure that the weights could not fall on her feet when the stick broke.

She wrote her results in a table.

Stick	Number of weights to break the stick
A	3
B	6
C	2
D	4

Remember

You can test different **materials** to find out which is the best one for the job. To do a **fair test** you must only change one thing each time.

Test yourself

1. In Oliver and Zoë's test, which fabric let the most water through?
2. **a** Which fabric would be best for a waterproof coat?
   b Explain why you chose this fabric.
3. Write down one thing that Oliver and Zoë kept the same each time to make their test fair.
4. Look at the table showing Molly's test results. Draw a block diagram to show what she found out. Start it like this.

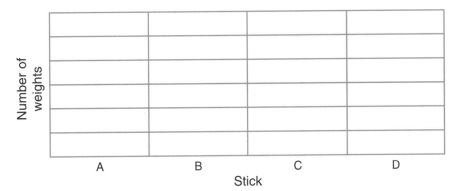

5. In Molly's test, which stick was the strongest?

Changing shapes

We can change the shape of some **materials** by squashing, bending, twisting or stretching them.

Changing the shape of clay

This ball of **clay** can be squashed to make it flatter.

It can be stretched to make it longer.

Clay can be twisted and bent.

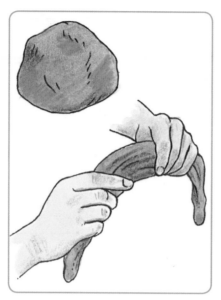

It is quite easy to change the shape of some materials like this, but it is very difficult to change the shape of other materials.

Easy to change the shape	Very difficult to change the shape
clay	metal
sponge	wood
foam	stone
elastic bands	glass

Test yourself

1. How could you make an elastic band longer?
2. Which materials can you change the shape of easily?
3. Which materials is it difficult to change the shape of?
4. Grace made a table like the one above, but she put clay in both columns. Why do you think she did this?

Remember

You can change the shape of some **materials** by squashing, stretching, bending and twisting.

Measuring

When you investigate a scientific question, you may need to measure something. You need different kinds of equipment for measuring different things.

When you write down a measurement it is very important to include the units. Saying that a **plant** is 10 tall does not really mean anything – you need to say 10 centimetres tall or 10 metres tall.

Length

Muhammad is measuring how tall his plants are. He is using a ruler to measure a length.

If you are measuring bigger things, you may need to use a tape measure.

The units for length are centimetres (cm) or metres (m).

Time

Poppy is finding out how long it takes water to drip through a piece of **fabric**. She is using a stopwatch to measure time.

The units for time are seconds (s), minutes (min) or hours (h).

Capacity

Charlie is watering some plants. He measures the amount of water he gives them using a measuring jug.

You can also measure **capacity** using a beaker.

The units for capacity are millilitres (ml) or litres (l).

Test yourself

1. **a** What equipment would you use to measure the length of your classroom?
   b What units would you write down next to your measurement?
2. What equipment would you use to find out how long you can hold your breath?
3. What units do you use for measuring capacity?

Remember

You must choose the most suitable equipment for your **investigation**.

You must write down units when you record measurements.

Recording

When you carry out an **investigation**, you need to record your **evidence**. You can do this using a table.

Jayden asked people what their favourite **fruit** was. He recorded his evidence in a table.

The top row tells you what the words or numbers underneath mean.

These are the different kinds of fruit that people liked.

Fruit	Number of people who liked this fruit best
apple	8
pear	4
banana	7
orange	2

Sometimes it is easier to see patterns in results if you use a **pictogram** or a **block diagram**.

Block diagram

A block diagram is a way of recording evidence using one square to show each person or thing.

This is a block diagram showing Jayden's evidence.

Each block shows one person who likes that fruit best.

Title

Favourite fruit

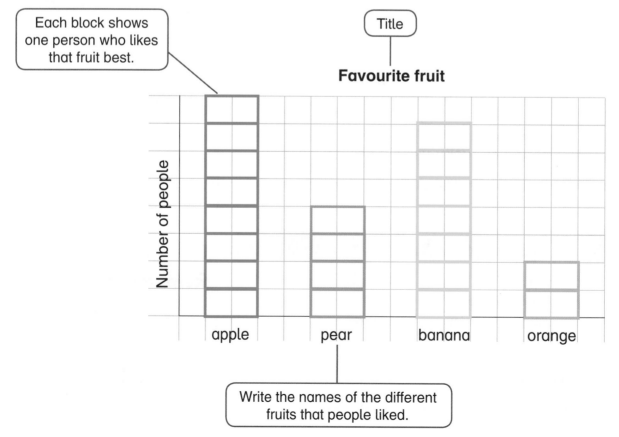

Write the names of the different fruits that people liked.

Pictogram

A pictogram is a way of recording evidence, using a small picture to show each person or thing.

This is a pictogram of Jayden's evidence.

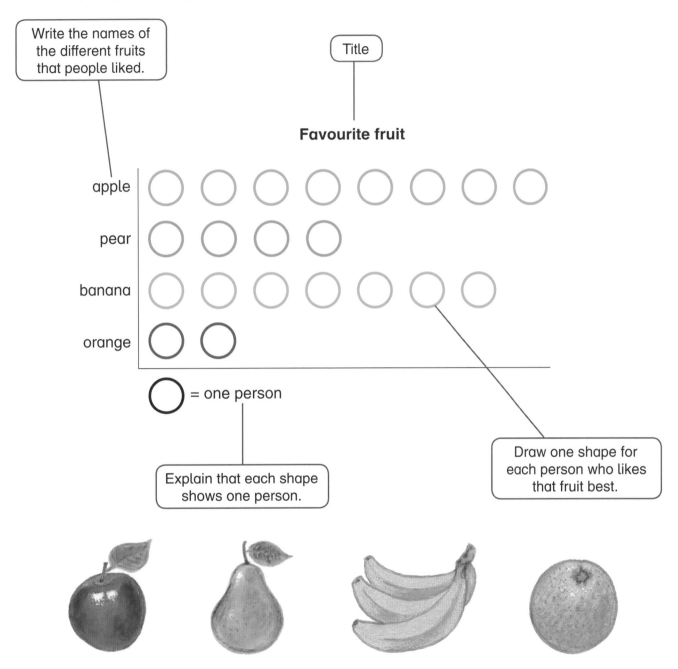

Write the names of the different fruits that people liked.

Title

Favourite fruit

apple

pear

banana

orange

◯ = one person

Explain that each shape shows one person.

Draw one shape for each person who likes that fruit best.

Test yourself

1. Shiv asked 20 people what their favourite drink was:
   - 10 people said they liked lemonade best
   - 5 people liked tea
   - 4 people liked coffee
   - 1 person liked water.

   Draw a table to show Shiv's evidence.

2. Draw a pictogram to show Shiv's evidence.

Remember

You can record **evidence** in a table. You can show evidence in a **pictogram**, where each picture means one thing. You can also show evidence in **block diagrams**.

Answers

Page 5
1 non-living
2 any three examples of animals or plants
3 A stone has never been alive. It does not grow, move or reproduce.

Page 6
1 grass, daisies, dandelions, daffodils (or any other plants that grow in the park)
2 any five of these animals: worms, bees, birds, snails, caterpillars, woodlice (or any other animals that live in the park)
3 worms (or any other animal that lives in the soil in the park)

Page 7
1 squirrels, woodpeckers, rabbits, insects (or any other animals that live in the wood)
2 any five of these plants: holly trees, beech trees, oak trees, blackberry bushes, ferns, bluebells (or any other plants that grow in the wood)
3 any three of these animals: woodlice, bees, snails, worms, rabbits, insects (or any other animals that live in dark habitats)

Page 8
1 so they can eat the leaves
2 It is damp in the wood.
3 Yes – they can build their nests in the trees or bushes.

Page 9
1 waterweed
2 tadpole
3 perch, pike
4 wheat → human

Page 10
1 any two of the plants shown on page 10 (or any other plants that you know)
2 They make seeds.
3 Plants all have green parts and they all have leaves. They all grow, move and reproduce.

4 any two of these differences: the cherry tree is much bigger than a daisy; the cherry tree has a trunk and the daisy does not; the daisy does not make cherries; the daisy has leaves on the ground and the cherry tree has leaves above the ground.

Page 11
1

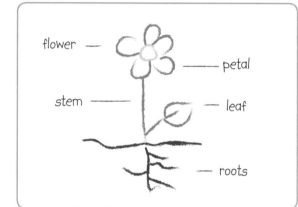

2 a trunk, branches

Page 13
1 carrots (or any other food plant)
2 any two of these plants: daffodils, grass, daisies, carrots (or any other garden plants)
3 deciduous
4 **a** no **b** yes **c** no

Page 15
1 any two of these plants: dandelion, horse chestnut tree, apple tree, tulip (or any other plants that grow from seeds)
2 daffodils, tulips, onions (or any other plants that grow from bulbs)
3 seeds
4 inside flowers or fruits
5 the pips (seeds)

Page 17
1 water
2 She used the same kind of seeds, she kept them in the same kind of containers, and she gave them all water.

Page 19

1 water, light and warmth
2 It gets taller, its stem gets wider and it grows more leaves.
3 They get very tall and thin and do not have many leaves. They are very pale.
4 They go brown and fall over.
5 He put both pots in the same place (so they both got the same amount of light). He only changed the amount of water the plants got.

Page 21

1 any four of the animals shown on page 21 (or any other animals that you know)
2 sparrows, robins, ducks (or any other birds)
3 sharks, sticklebacks (or any other fish)
4 Animals can all grow, move and reproduce.
5 any two of these differences: crocodiles have four legs and humans only have two; crocodiles have scaly skin and humans do not; crocodiles have much bigger mouths than humans; crocodiles live in water and humans do not; crocodiles and humans eat different things.

Page 23

1 crocodiles, snakes (or any other reptiles)
2 frogs, newts (or any other amphibians)
3 You could have written some of these similarities: they are both mammals; they both have hair or fur; they are both omnivores.
4 They eat plants and animals.
5 a herbivores b omnivores c carnivores

Page 25

1 a calf
2 fish and amphibians
3 You could have written down some of these animals: humans, blackbirds, cats, dogs, sheep, cows.

Page 27

1 humans, pandas, cows, dogs, cats (or any other mammals)
2 ducks, flamingos (or any other birds)
3 frogs (tadpoles) and butterflies (caterpillars)
4 a frog
5 a butterfly

Page 29

1 any five of these body parts: head, hair, mouth, face, neck, arm, elbow, wrist, hand, finger, thumb, leg, knee, ankle, foot, toe (or any other body parts)
2 sight, hearing, smell, taste, touch
3 your skin

Page 31

1 A baby cannot do anything for itself.
2 You could have written down any three of these things: you can walk, talk, feed yourself, wash yourself, put your own clothes on, read and write.
3 Your parents or carers give you food to eat. They have a home for you to live in. They make sure you have enough clean clothes.
4 You will get taller and heavier. You will be able to have babies of your own.
5 You will still have two eyes and two ears, a nose and a mouth. You will still have the same colour eyes. There are lots of other ways that you will stay the same.

Page 33

1 You will die.
2 any three of these foods: bread, rice, pasta, cereals
3 chocolate, ice cream, fizzy drinks (or any other sugary foods)
4 eat the right kinds of food, exercise and keep yourself clean
5 hot and tired
6 a You may have written that you should eat more fruit and vegetables.
  b You may have written that you should eat fewer sweets and cakes.

Page 35

1 summer
2 winter
3 summer
4 autumn

Page 37

1 any three of these things: saucepans, coins, cars, table legs, spoons (or any other metal objects)
2 any three of these things: umbrellas, toys, cups (or any other plastic objects)
3 cotton and wool
4 any three of these materials: pottery, metal, plastic, paper
5 any three of these materials: wood, paper, cardboard, cotton, wool

Page 39

1 You could have written some of these words: shiny, hard, stiff, smooth.
2 You could have written some of these words: transparent, hard, stiff, smooth.
3 You could have written some of these words: rough, hard, dull.
4 any three of these materials: brick, metal, stone, glass (or any other hard materials)
5 any three of these materials: metal, glass, plastic, rubber. (Some kinds of stone are also waterproof.)

Page 41

1 Wood is strong and stiff.
2 Wood is strong and stiff, and it looks nice.
3 Wool is soft, bendy and keeps us warm.
4 Fabric is soft and bendy, and cotton soaks up water.
5 Fabric is soft and bendy and it looks nice.
6 Iron is strong and stiff.

Page 43

1 the blue fabric
2 a the yellow fabric
  b It did not let any water through.
3 You could have written that they poured the same amount of water on each fabric or that they counted the drops that went through in one minute for each fabric.

4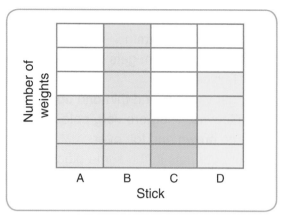

5 Stick B

Page 44

1 stretch it (pull it)
2 clay, sponge, foam, elastic bands (or any other materials that are easy to bend)
3 metal, wood, stone, glass (or any other materials that are difficult to bend)
4 Clay is hard and stiff after it has been heated.

Page 45

1 a tape measure
  b metres and/or centimetres
2 stopwatch
3 litres or millilitres

Page 47

1

Drink	Number of people who liked this drink best
lemonade	10
tea	5
coffee	4
water	1

2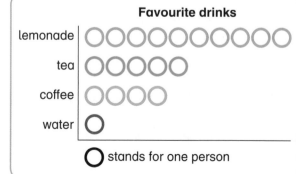

Glossary

absorbent	a **material** that soaks up something, such as a cloth soaks up water
adult	a **human** or **animal** that is old enough to have babies
amphibians	**animals** with moist skin that lay **eggs** in water
animals	**living** things that can move around
autumn	the **season** when days are getting shorter and the weather is getting colder
birds	**animals** with beaks, wings and feathers that lay **eggs** with hard shells
block diagram	a way of recording **evidence** using one square to show each person or thing
brick	a hard, baked **clay** block used to make buildings and walls
bulb	an underground part of some **plants** such as daffodils
capacity	how much something holds: capacity is measured in millilitres and litres
cardboard	thick or stiff **paper**
carnivore	an **animal** that eats only other animals
caterpillar	a small **animal** that eats **leaves**, and turns into a butterfly
chrysalis	the covering of a **caterpillar** while it is turning into a butterfly
clay	a **material** that is found in the ground, which can be made into different shapes and heated to make it hard and stiff
cotton	a thread made from a cotton **plant** that can be woven into cloth
deciduous	trees that lose their **leaves** in **winter**
egg	something laid by **birds**, **fish**, **amphibians** or **reptiles** for their babies to grow inside
evergreen	trees that keep their **leaves** all year around
evidence	measurements you make or things you **observe** in an **investigation**
exercise	moving around, such as running or swimming
fabric	cloth or knitted **wool** that clothes can be made from
fair test	an **investigation** where you only change one thing and keep all the other things the same
fins	parts of a **fish** that help them to swim
fish	**animals** with **fins** and wet **scales** that lay **eggs** in water
flower	part of a **plant** that **seeds** grow from
food chain	a way of showing what eats what
fruit	something that surrounds **seeds**, which **humans** like to eat
glass	a hard, **transparent material** used to make windows and drinking glasses
habitat	the place where an organism lives
hearing	the **sense** that allows you to hear sounds with your ears
herbivore	an **animal** that eats only **plants**
human	an **animal** like you
hygiene	keeping yourself clean
investigation	finding an answer to a scientific question
leaves	green, flat parts of **plants**

living	a thing that can grow, move and **reproduce**
mammals	**animals** with hair or fur that have babies that look like their parents
materials	everything is made of a material – **glass**, **wood** and **metal** are all different materials
metal	a strong and shiny **material** such as iron or gold
micro-habitat	a very small **habitat**, such as the soil under a **stone**
non-living	something that is not alive and has never been alive
observe	to look carefully at something during an **investigation**
omnivore	an **animal** that eats **plants** and other animals
opaque	a **material** that blocks light, so an opaque material causes a shadow
paper	a thin **material** made from **wood**
pictogram	a way of recording **evidence**, using a small picture to show each person or thing
plants	**living** things that have green parts and cannot move around
plastic	a light and strong **material** used to make many different objects
pottery	objects such as plates and mugs made out of baked **clay**
reproduce	when **animals** or **plants** make new **young**
reptiles	**animals** with dry **scales** that lay **eggs** on land
rock	a hard **material** that comes from the ground
root	the part of a **plant** that is in the soil
rubber	a stretchy and strong **material** that is used to make rubber bands
scales	tiny plates that cover the skin of **fish** and **reptiles**
seasons	**spring**, **summer**, **autumn** and **winter**
seeds	parts of a **plant** that can grow into new plants. **Fruit** seeds are sometimes called pips.
senses	**sight**, **hearing**, **touch**, **smell** and **taste**
sight	the **sense** that lets you see things with your eyes
smell	the **sense** that allows you to smell things with your nose
spring	the **season** when days are getting longer and the weather is getting warmer
stem	part of a **plant** that holds up the **leaves** and **flowers**
stone	a small piece of **rock**
summer	the **season** with the longest days and warmest weather
tadpole	a tadpole is a baby frog but it does not look like a frog. It grows legs and loses its tail when it gets older.
taste	the **sense** that lets you taste things with your tongue
touch	the **sense** that lets you feel things with your skin
transparent	see-through
trunk	a very stiff **stem** that trees have
waterproof	a waterproof **material** is a material that does not let water go through it
winter	the **season** with the shortest days and coldest weather
wood	a strong and stiff **material** that we get from trees
wool	the soft hair of sheep that can be used to make clothes
young	small **animals** that will grow up into **adults**